Dreaming the
End of War

Other Books by Benjamin Alire Sáenz

POETRY
Elegies in Blue
Dark and Perfect Angels
Calendar of Dust

FICTION
In Perfect Light
Sammy and Juliana in Hollywood
The House of Forgetting
Carry Me Like Water
Flowers for the Broken

CHILDREN'S BOOKS
A Perfect Season for Dreaming
Grandma Fina and Her Wonderful Umbrellas
A Gift from Papá Diego

Dreaming the End of War

POEMS

Benjamin Alire Sáenz

COPPER CANYON PRESS

Cover art: *By the Side of the Road*, 1998. Monoprint by Denny Moers.

Copper Canyon Press is in residence at Fort Worden State Park in Port Townsend, Washington, under the auspices of Centrum Foundation. Centrum is a gathering place for artists and creative thinkers from around the world, students of all ages and backgrounds, and audiences seeking extraordinary cultural enrichment.

LIBRARY OF CONGRESS CATALOGING-IN-PUBLICATION DATA
Sáenz, Benjamin Alire.
  Dreaming the end of war / by Benjamin Alire Sáenz.
      p. cm.
   ISBN 1-55659-239-6 (pbk. : alk. paper)
   I. Mexican-American Border Region—Poetry. 2. Mexican Americans—Poetry. I. Title.
   PS3569.A27D74 2006
   811'.54—DC22

2005030742

98765432   FIRST PRINTING

COPPER CANYON PRESS
Post Office Box 271
Port Townsend, Washington 98368
www.coppercanyonpress.org

In Memory of my father

Juan Villanueva Sáenz

February 20, 1929–August 2, 2003

I remember him rising in the middle of the night to water
the cotton fields. I remember the day he came home from
a place where he went to get healed of his alcoholism. I
remember hugging him and smelling him and looking up
at him, and seeing hope written on his face . . .

Hope is an instinct only the reasoning human mind can kill.
An animal never knows despair.

—GRAHAM GREENE

Dreaming the
End of War

Do Not Mind the Bombs

        In Belgium, I remember
they called this day *White Monday*. Belgium was my
home when I was learning words like *God*
and *doubt* and *faith*. Belgium was my home
when I entered the country called *Man*. There,
in that land where I'd learned to fall in love
with learning, winter always stayed and stayed,
the days too dark, the rains incessant, pounding,
pounding—and all the sleepers dreamed of sun
and shirtless days. Shirtless, shoeless days.
I remember: trains, leaves, trees. Remember
too that aging, tired woman who'd told me why
the trees grew straight and tall *in rows*
in Belgium's rain-soaked earth.
        I remember what she'd said: "The trees,
we planted them in rows. When the war
was finally won." I pictured her young,
a handsome husband at her side. At last the war
was done! At last! And before they planted crops,
they planted trees—the trees the war had stolen
from the earth. "What the bombs had not destroyed,
we chopped for fuel. Their stumps and branches
gave us warmth. The land was bare and spent.
The earth, it reeked of guns and blood and rotting
flesh. And so we planted trees. And as we worked
we found reminders of the war. A rifle, empty
shells, the remains of a man, a bullet through
his chest, his uniform turning to dust. We called
the priest and blessed the bones. A boy! I knew

he'd been a boy. Belgian, English, French! Bah!
He was a boy! I cried that night for all
the world had lost—then woke and finished
planting. And through the years, we watched
the growing trees. Before my mother died, she went
from tree to tree, kissing leaves and branches.
'Have you gone mad?' I yelled. And she screamed
back: 'I am, at last, in love!' She smelled of leaves
and bark the night she breathed her last. The day I buried
her, I leaned against a tree and wept. I swear, *I swear*
I smelled her breath as I leaned against that tree."

     Today, I hear that woman's voice as I
read the morning news—the news of bombs,
of all the deaths, Americans, Iraqis, children, women,
men. Dead. Like π the blood and bodies
run into infinity. I walk outside, the sky as clear
as simple boyhood words *mamá, papá, y agua*. Oh
for a day when this would be my only task—to sit
and memorize the blueness of a sky.
     Better now to study
trees that grow on desert sands than to study war.
So I begin to count the leaves on limbs
of waking trees. I know that wars are raging
everywhere. Even in my heart. *Do not mind*
the bombs. Do not mind them, not today.
     I wander through my yard,
examining the plants. I lost some to the freeze—but
most survived. I touch and kiss the tender leaves
and speak to them, half lost, half crazed,
and half expecting trees and plants
and shrubs to kiss me back. Perhaps, today,
they'll kiss me back. I touch a desert bush—yellow
flowers bursting like a flame, spring's first blaze

of light. The dog running up and down and up
and down the yard, then rolling on the grass
to scratch her back. I laugh and speak
to her. The wars are everywhere. I'll plant
another tree. Something to survive the torture
of the sun. Something to withstand a thousand
years of drought.

       I touch a tree I planted
years ago. I touch and touch. *Oh, do not mind
the bombs today. Kiss me, kiss me back.*

The First Dream:
Learning to Kill

The *curanderos say*
                    the animals will save us
in the end. *Be good to animals.*

Esos inocentes son la salvación
del mundo. They will be waiting

when you die. When I
                    was a boy, my violence
was sweet, uncomplicated. I spent

hours blowing up
                    ants with Black Cats,
those small, elegant firecrackers

patterned after TNT.
                    But ants were not
the only creatures I set out

to destroy. Daily, on that
                    farm I learned
the meaning of the simple

joy of killing. That is when

you were heard. When you killed. That
is when you were most alive. *¡Oiganme!*
¿Que no me conocen? ¡Quiero que
me oigan! ¡Estoy aqui gritando
todos los nombres del mundo! Killing.

The only road to take

killing, the only way

to use your body

the only way to use

your imagination,

the only way to learn

how to become

hard in the same way
                the land was hard
hard even though it was

soft in certain places
               but that softness
could fool you, *hard*

I'm yelling now! Hard!
                the land could be harder
than my father's hazel gaze

harder than Aztec stone
              and every day a woman
or her son or her husband broke

in half as if they were nothing
              more than dry
mesquite, broke

in half, broke

a man broke

a woman broke

or their son broke

in half

trying to soften an earth
                    that fought back because
it was as alive as anything

that walked on two legs, refusing

to be domesticated as if

it were an ox or a mule or

one of San Isidro's docile angels.

The earth refused
                    to make
an easy peace

with those who claimed
                    to own it. The earth,
in its stubborn intelligence,

refused to learn
                    our rituals and our
language, and I

wanted to be as stubborn

                as hard, as illiterate

and intelligent

as the earth. As the good

                earth. But I held

only the small and intimate

knowledge that a farm

teaches a boy.

But even with my limited

and provincial education

I understood

what the boys

in New York and L.A.

and Boston and Chicago

understood—that

                killing was part of what it meant

to live. And I wanted to live

so I killed

and not only ants but

                nests full of wasps

and birds, killed them with BB guns

and once I plotted to kill

a cat (it was mangy

and mean anyway) but

I never carried out

my plan, but in my heart
                          I'd killed that cat
Killed and killed that cat

and killed and killed
rat-tat-tat-tat-tat-tat-tat
and in my heart I killed
rat-tat-tat-tat-tat-tat-tat

my brothers more than once
I killed, I killed, I killed
Rat-tat-tat-tat-tat
Rat-tat-tat-tat-tat
I killed my brothers

I killed my brothers

I killed my brothers

in my heart and in my mind
                          over and over and over
and as we shot each other

with those plastic bazookas
                    we'd begged my father for
Dad, bazookas! begged because

we loved *Rat Patrol* and *Combat!*
                    and all the other war
shows on TV they invented just

for us—the children of the nation—

for us so we could begin to love

guns and the Constitution and our rights

to kill game for sport, killing, fathers

and mothers approving

because we were boys
                    and it did not matter
that we were Mexican boys

because in matters of killing
                    gender takes precedence
over race, ethnicity, and national

origin. So I watched television
                    and all the old movies
where handsome white men

spoke the American idiom

as if their tongues were doing

a graceful Southern waltz,

handsome white men who

made the Japanese and Germans bleed.

The enemy didn't even sound human

when they died. Stubborn
                              even in death, the enemy
refused to die in English.

And so I pretended
                              my brothers were
Japanese and Germans,

ripe for killing, even though I knew
                              they were only Mexicans
like me. But in my head

they deserved a bad end
                              they were Mexicans
and neutral in the war.

How could you be neutral
                              with Hitler on
the loose like the devil

in the book of Job
                              going to and fro
upon the earth, *the Mexicans*

neutral, and my brothers
                    Mexicans—every
single one of them

and it was up to me to exact
                    revenge, up to me
to make them bleed

for sins against the nation
                    the offices we hold are
mostly self-appointed.

I knew the blackness of Cain
                    without ever knowing
the innocence of Abel

but original sin has always
                    mattered more than
original innocence

in the theology handed down

by grandmothers and grandfathers

who were taught to hate themselves

by a nation   and a faith

that could spit

rivers on their faces

I wondered why God

did not strike me down

in the same way I killed

ants and wasps and birds.

The Second Dream:
Killing and Memory and War

I was against the war
in Vietnam.
In this, I was not
original.
What did I know? At sixteen?
And seventeen? And eighteen?
What did I know?
And the men who died?

What did they know?

*

Augustine argued for the notion
of a *just war.* But there were
certain requirements.
Most of us who speak
of justice and wars
have never bothered to examine
Augustine's words.
In the age of information, we choose
to live without information.

*

I am not a historian.
I am not a philosopher.
I have abandoned
my identity
as a theologian,
and my identity as a writer
is useless

in the face of the many aggressions
that surround
the globe
like the barbed wire
around a concentration camp.

✢

There are thousands of generals
throughout the history
of this beautiful and sad
and tragic earth
who have believed the wars
they waged were just.
                    Some of these generals
were readers of Augustine. Some of them
only pretended to have read what
he had to say about the waging of wars.
All of them died believing
that the young men who bled
to death on battlefields
under their command
were purified, made holy

by the blood of the bullets
that ripped them apart
as if they were made only of paper.

They might as well have died on a cross.

✢

We live by the sword. Then
damn it to hell, let us die

by the sword. And cut
the whining. Be a man.

*

My uncle Frank told me the peace sign
was the footprint of the American chicken.
My uncle Frank never fought in a war.

*

The living cry that the wars they fight are just.
The dead answer that they *are not.*
The living think the dead are confused.

*

There are voices in my
head. They come to me
at odd hours and whisper
their chaos in my ear.
I remain mostly unmoved.
I know the voices are trying
to seduce me, take away
what little order I have left.

War is institutionalized murder.

War is menstruation envy.

*Wars, like acts of nature,
have enabled us to keep
in check the human
population of the earth.*

War is not good for trees.
War is not good for flowers.

I am a mathematician. I beg
you. No math for war.

Blood, blood, blood
makes the grass grow.
If Hitler were alive, he would
kill all Mexicans.

If we had camps for Jews
and camps for Indians
and camps for Japanese
and camps for braceros
and camps for Mexicans
fleeing the Revolution
then why can't we have
camps for Arabs?

Hitler is alive and living
in my heart.

I am a poet. I beg
you. No words for war

☆

I know a good man. Another
man with the same name
was killed in Vietnam. When
I read the name I thought
of the good man I know
and wondered about the dead
soldier *was he a good man, too?*

＊

My uncle asked me if I was a pacifist.
I knew that my heart was too angry,
would strike back if provoked,
a genetic reflex. I looked my uncle
straight in the eyes and said *yes.*

＊

I have learned and forgotten, learned
and forgotten all the details of the war
between Palestinians and Israelis, of why they hate
each other and why there can be no peace.

I know it all goes back to the land.

Even though I am a Catholic, I have failed
to keep up with the wars between my fellow
Catholics and Protestants in Northern Ireland
and all the nuances and all the groups, the IRA
and Unionists and Sinn Fein and bloody
English bastards and colonialism and the history
of how one people subjugates another people
and the thousand different ways the history
of subjugation is interpreted by the current
populace. I understand loss and how a bullet
cuts through a family and how that bullet
becomes the air we live and breathe.
I understand these shadows, and how
these shadows become a politics
and how that politics becomes a flag
and how that flag becomes the only house
we live in. I can touch these shadows—
even if I never come to understand

the nuances and complicated matters
of why there is still blood on
the ancient cobblestone streets. Even
in the bright light of day, there are angry
phantoms that run through the hearts of all
of us. Who can claim *my heart is pure?*
I keep thinking everything, *everything*
in the world goes back to the land.

I don't remember why the Walloons
and the Flemish have been warring
for thousands of years in Belgium.
Four years I lived in that blessèd
country of rain yet never
understood the hate. I remember being
told it had something to do with the land.

I have stopped hoping all this will end.
Killing in the name of the land is a habit,
an art, a discipline, the great addiction
of every civilization that has ever had
any claim to greatness.

*

It was a graceful thing, to blow up
a hill of ants, to watch a bird fall
to earth. I have never killed
another man. I don't know
if men die graceful as birds. To kill
a man. Like my uncle, I have never
been to war. My knowledge
of these things is limited—though
my imagination can be as savage

as that of any other man who's ever
felt rage running through his veins.
I no longer plot to kill cats,
though I am still stepping on ants
and the occasional cockroach that
invades my house. This may have
something to do   with the land.

The Third Dream:
The Names and Their Gods

Day after day, I hear stories of the men and women

Who were killed, stories of women and men

Who left final messages of love through the miracle

Of cell phones. Hour after hour, I see pictures of survivors

Weeping bitterly on the streets. I see footage of the wreckage,

See faces on the screen, faces of husbands, hoping for news

Of a wife *married only six months*, faces of fathers trying to hide

Their rage and grief as they search for a son *he was only twenty-four.*

Months later, I am still reading paragraphs and poems about

The dead, their pictures in newsprint. The word *resurrection*

Appears in my mind as the words *The End* appear on a screen

When a movie is over. I begin to whisper words to myself

Until the words become a chant *Americans, Israelis, Palestinians.*

Americans, Israelis, Palestinians. Arabs, Jews, Catholics, Muslims.

Protestants, Jews, Muslims. Abraham, Muhammad, Jesus. Koran,

Gospels, Torah. Koran, Gospels, Torah. Blood, death, hate. Blood,

Jesus, Muhammad. Death, Catholics, Torah. Israelis, Gospel, Hate.

New York, New York. Pilgrims. Immigrants. Mecca. Blood, Jerusalem,

Jerusalem, next year in Jerusalem. The words become a litany—then

Run into one another until they become lost, until

All the beautiful words destroy one another, until there is only

One word left standing, *Resurrection.* The word sounds like

The last column holding up the Acropolis, the name for the last

Shovel digging up the dead: *wake, breathe, live.* But I know this is

A dream that will never come to pass. I know it is easy

For me to dream these things because I am sitting in the comfort

Of my office. Because I am not a Jew. Because I am not a Palestinian.

Because I do not live in the shadow of guns. Because

The guns are not pointing at me. I know this is a dream

That will never come to be because I hear people say *all*

Of this, it is because of the Jews. I hear people say *we must shut*

Down every mosque. The mosques are filled with terrorists. And because

I am a Catholic, I think of all the Catholic churches

in the New World. I think of the Mayan libraries, burned

To the ground, the temples and cities of the Aztecs leveled

To dust. I think of the Incan roads, of Machu Picchu.

I think that killing has been made too easy—it has

Always been too easy. I think you should be forced

To know the name of a man before you spill his blood, know

The name of his wife and the names of each of her daughters

And sons. I think the names of the dead should appear

On the walls of every church, synagogue, and mosque. I know

There must be a definition for terrorism just as there must be

A definition for love just as there must be a definition for *enough.*

I try to imagine the names of all who have been killed. I try

To imagine their gods. I try to imagine their gardens. I try to

Imagine their kitchens, the foods they cooked, the spices, the table,

The prayers, the smells of a living house. I shut myself into

A room and begin writing paragraphs. One paragraph for each

Life. I spend hours in solitude writing elegies to the dead,

Spelling their names in English, in Hebrew, in Arabic. I begin

Writing definitions for words that will save them all. Then

I despair. And then the word for resurrection disappears. I let

out something that resembles a cry. And I know I am lost. I am lost.

The Fourth Dream:
Families and Flags and Revenge

My niece, thirteen years old,
shot in the back of the head, executed
in some barbaric ritual. For years
I've fought thinking of her final seconds,
what she must have thought, prayed for,
if she begged *please* at the hour of her death.
Without the unwelcome intervention
of these bastards, today she would be
a woman. She might be a mother, might be
holding a son in her arms as her mother
held her. They have never caught
the men who killed this girl, this girl who
scarred my sister's heart, this girl who
lit our family's flame as if we were a candle
that belonged only on the altar
that was her face.

                              Once,
I dreamed I found these men. I woke
searching for a gun, could feel
the spit in my throat. I knew
that spit to be the only weapon
I could call my own.

I cannot say what I would
say or feel or do if these men, these sons
of bitches who live on with the blood
of my blood on their hands,
were caught, prosecuted, found
guilty, sentenced to death, injected
with something more elegant
than bullets in our own graceless ritual

of revenge. I do not know what kind
of river would run through me
as I saw their limp bodies lying
there like the slaughtered
deer of my childhood, killed
by the state in my name.
Killed by the state in the name of my sister's
grief, in the name of my mother's tears,
in the name of that awful day when
rage cut through a household like
a pair of scissors cutting up the sun,
leaving us all in a darkness
whose cold shadow we still feel
even in the warmest days of summer.

*

In a photograph at the National Gallery,
in the capital city of my nation, a soldier
is holding another sobbing soldier
in his arms. We are to understand that there
has been a battle. We are to understand
that some have been killed. We are to
understand that the men are
on Korean soil. The solider who is
sobbing, burying his head deep
into the shoulder of his comrade,
looks like a boy. *Must be a boy.*
The older soldier (who looks as if there
is still a boy living inside him) is trying
to keep the younger man—the man
who is sobbing—from breaking. That is
why he is holding him. But I think once
war has entered and broken a man, he
will always be broken.

There is another man in the photograph.
He is not looking at the two men. Instead
he is looking down as if he is reading.
Perhaps he is embarrassed to see a man
holding another man. Perhaps he is reading
a pocket Bible or the Book of Hours, thanking
God he is alive. Perhaps whatever he reads
keeps him sane or keeps him from admitting
that he has seen so many men die that he has
stopped grieving for them and cannot even
bring himself to hate those who would kill
him tomorrow. Or perhaps he no longer
has the patience for young men who do not
understand the nature of war. *What did you*
think you came here to do? Or perhaps he is tirelessly
reading and rereading a letter from home—
and that is where he is, home, kissing
his wife, telling her in between all his hungry
kisses, telling her that killing has taught
him to love. Finally, he has learned
to love. He can taste the irony
in the meat loaf his wife
has cooked for him.

The taste will never leave his mouth.

*

In the South there are those

who are obsessed with the Confederacy,
with the battles and the names
and the graves. They carry the taste
of that treason on their tongues

as if it were a Communion wafer.
There is no repentance—there is only
regret that the war was lost.
They would take up arms again.
Oh, for another chance to win
that war the second time around.

✳

I have never been nostalgic
for slave cultures. Neither Greece nor
Rome, nor the American South.

✳

Remember Pearl Harbor!
Remember the Maine!
Remember Sacco and Vanzetti!

Those who forget are shallow;
people who keep things wallow
in the forest of bitterness.

Remember the Scottsboro Boys!
Remember the Alamo!
Haymarket! Remember Haymarket!

Some days I prefer the shallowness.
You must remember this, a kiss is . . .
Other days, I bathe in bitterness.
Remember, man, that you are dust
and to dust you shall return you must
remember this and to dust and to dust

✳

I don't believe a flag
is important

enough to kiss—
or even burn.

Some men would hate me
enough to kill me
if they read these words.

The Fifth Dream:
Bullets and Deserts and Borders

A man is walking toward me.
He is alone.
He has been walking through the desert.
He has been walking for days.
He has been walking for years.
His lips are dry
and cracking
like a piece of spent soil.
I can see his open wounds.
His eyes are dark
as a Tanzanian night.

He discovers I have been watching
though he has long ceased to care
what others see. I ask him
his name, ask him what
has brought him here, ask
him to name
his angers and his loves.
                    He opens his mouth
to speak—
but just as his words hit
the air, a bullet
pierces his heart.

                    I do not know
the country
of this man's birth. I only know
that he is from
the desert. He has the worn

look of despair
that only rainless days can give.
That is all I know.
He might have been born
in Jerusalem. He might have been
born in Egypt. He might
have been the direct descendant
of a pharaoh. His name
might have been Ptolemy.
His name might have been
Moses. Or Jesus.
Or Muhammad.
He might have been a prophet.
He might have been a common thief.
He might have been a terrorist
or he might have been just
another man destined
to be worn down
by the ceaseless, callous storms.
He might have come
from a country called Afghanistan.
He might have been from Mexico.

He might have been
looking for a well.
His dreams were made of water.
His lips touching
water—yes—
that is what he was dreaming.

I can still hear the sound of the bullet.

*

The man reappears.
It does not matter
that I do not want him
in my dreams. He is
searching through the rubble
of what was once his house.
There are no tears on his
face. His lips still yearn
for water.

*

I wake. I begin to believe
that the man has escaped
from Auschwitz. Perhaps he sinned
against the Nazis or because
he was a collaborator or because
he was Jewish
or because he loved another man.
He has come
to the desert looking
for a place he can call home.
I fall asleep trying
to give the man a name.

*

The man is now
walking toward a city
that is no longer there.

*

I am the man.
I see clearly. I am
awake now.
It is me. It has taken me
a long time to know this.
I am a Palestinian.
I am an Israeli.
I am a Mexican.
I am an American.
I am a busboy in a tall building
that is about to collapse.
I am attending a Seder and I am
tasting my last bitter
herb. I am a boy who has learned
all his prayers. I am bowing
toward Mecca in a house
whose roof will soon collapse
on my small frame.
I am a servant. I shine shoes
and wash the feet
of the rich. I am an illegal.
I am a Mexican who hates all Americans.
I am an American who hates all Mexicans.
I am a Palestinian who hates all Israelis.
I am an Israeli who hates all Palestinians.
I am a Palestinian Jew who hates himself.

I am dying of all this knowledge.
I am dying of thirst.
I am a river that will never know water again.
I am becoming dust.

*

I am walking toward my home.
Mexico City? Washington?
Mecca? Jerusalem?
I don't know. I don't know.

*

I am walking in the desert.

I see that I am reaching a border.

A bullet is piercing my heart.

The Sixth Dream:
Animals, Food, Aesthetics

My father never
>
> took me hunting.

In this way, he exiled me
>
> from manhood.

My mother did not allow him
>
> to keep his rifle in the house.

>
> *

The first time I saw a dead
>
> deer hanging upside down

I hated my father, my uncles,
>
> hated the beer on their breath,

The smell of dead animal
>
> all over them. (I have always

Wondered why men smell
>
> like the things they kill just

As I have always wondered
>
> why they smell like the women

They love. The things they
>
> kill. The women they love.)

>
> *

When you butcher a hog
>
> you have to castrate him first.

If you don't

        the meat will be poisoned, no

Good for eating.

        A pig squeals

When you shoot it

        but then it stops

And there is quiet.

        I've seen a whole hog

Being cut up

        to all its edible parts.

*

I've seen men cut the throats of goats and sheep.
I've seen chickens with their heads wrung off.
This was not done for sport.
This was done for eating.
We lived on a farm.
We were never hungry.

I sometimes imagine scenes from
my childhood at the grocery store,
the glassy eyes of animals following
me as I search the meat section
at my local grocery store. I think about
lifeless animals, how they hang
limp, how the blood
spills out where the knife first cuts
like water bursting from a dam.
I always promised I would look
away. But, when the next time

arrived, I always watched, then told
myself I watched as punishment—
atonement for the sin we were committing.
I will refuse to eat. Always I ate.
And ate. I once made this confession
to the priest. He whispered that I should
pray to Saint Francis, who would guide
me to holiness. But Saint Francis never
explained why animals, when
they were alive, did not look like food.

*

I live in the century of aesthetics.

*

Though I can take a thought and dress it up
Then take it out to eat, and then pretend

That alexandrine couplets are my friends;
Alone, my thoughts are wrinkled and unpressed,

And I take off the clothes so I can rest—
My thoughts are more important than the dress.

*

Though I can take a word and make it rhyme,
I cannot shove the world into a couplet.

*

As I stare at a tightly packaged piece of meat,
inspected, accurately weighed and very nearly
bloodless, I stand in a clean aisle, shiny
floors you could eat off of, wondering if
the price is good, and wondering, too, how
we have managed to get rid of the odor of blood.

*

Glass slippers, far more precious than our feet.
An animal is nothing more than meat.

Neatly packaged.

I live in the century of aesthetics.

The Seventh Dream:
Resurrecting Dogs

Our dog, Buster, went missing for days.
My brothers and I called his name
for hours until our throats became deserts
of empty hope. We looked for him among
the tall rows of summer corn. We did not
let our mother comfort us. On that day
we learned the word *despair*. She saw
our tears though we refused to cry. We were
boys and lost without the solace
of a dog who was protector and companion,
a dog who loved far simpler than a mother
or a father or an uncle or an aunt.

           I don't remember how I heard
the news of Buster's fate, found shot
and buried, only his head sticking up
from the earth. I dreamed that dog's head
for weeks and thought I saw him once
in a painting by Goya (things
you lose have a way of returning
in unexpected places: grocery stores,
funerals, museums in Madrid). I have
often wondered about Buster's end
and what it was about a farm dog
that would drive a man to kill.

               My father lost
the farm, and I became a city boy.
And I have loved the city ever since.
I moved from place to place, itinerant

as a farmworker looking for seasonal
work or just a place to sleep. Leaving
home and hungry for the world, at last
I saw London, Rome, Paris. Dar es Salaam.
Copenhagen. The cities I wandered
made me feel small as a boy counting stars.

Somehow, by chance or by fortune
or by the design of my mother's God, I have
a house. *A house I tell you.* A house is a miracle
for a man who was born to wander. I have
a family, wife, daughter, backyard. *I want
a dog,* I begged my wife like a boy who'd
never left the farm, like a boy who'd lost
his faith and wanted to believe again
in resurrection. A year went by—then
she relented. We brought home a dog,
a dog! my boy-heart singing. Now
among my many duties on this earth
I am charged with caring for this dog. *Be good
to animals,* the curanderos say. *Esos inocenetes
son la salvación del mundo.*

The Eighth Dream:
Summer (and a Dog of My Own)

Once, I dreamed of having all of this. A wife,
a home, a dog, a yard, a writer's life.

I write at a desk that is mine, sit in a chair
that is mine, stare out at a garden that is mine.
I own rows and rows of books. In my
boyhood there were only rows of crops.

There is comfort in this life. I've worked
for this. And it did not come cheap. And yet
this summer brings no hint of peace.

A tightening, tightening of the fist. And no release.

*

I walk across the bridge—to go to Juárez.
There is no water running through the river.

If a river has no water, does it cease to be a river?
If a man has lost his heart, does he cease to be a man?

*

This room is where I come to read and write.
I thought that here, the world would disappear.
But these few months have brought me discontent.
A father who is ill. A mother who is tired. A brother
in trouble with the law. And when I look outside
my window, all I see is America sitting at a bar,
drinking and drinking and waiting for love, growing more
desperate as the clock ticks toward last call: *Tell me*

that you love me. Love me, love me, love me. My father
does not understand why his body no longer loves
him. My country does not understand why the world
does not admire its great and awesome beauty, *and I,*
I cannot understand the stream of my own thoughts
which empties out of me. I'm as sick as my father,
as drunk as America. My dreams are filled
with the remembered fragments of his life.
The shrapnel digs into my skin: an uncle returning
from a war, a boy tearing up a draft card, a soldier
playing taps, a woman who believes her screams
will resurrect the South. I begin to write down
the names of places as familiar to me as the troubled
lives of brothers who once shared a poor
and crowded house. The places shout their names
at me and they become clouds filling the empty
sky above me. I close my eyes and the places
are nothing now except seductive chaos.

> *Nicaragua Cuba Vietnam*
> *Panama Salvador Haiti*
> *Kuwait Afghanistan Iraq*
> *Korea Russia Guatemala*
> *Selma Hanoi Birmingham*
> *Manzanar Dachau El Mazote*
> *My Lai Abu Ghraib Tlatelolco*
> *Guantánamo Gountánamo Guantánamo*

I want to shut it all out, so I
begin listening to Louis Armstrong
as I drive through the desert
though I have no destination.
Louis is singing a song
about summer. The song makes

me want to stand still
because it is about love and silence
and everything in the song
is perfect and lyrical and lovely,
the way all songs and poems should be,
and I wish I had a music like that
inside me. And then Louis starts
singing about children fishing
and how a summer day is silent
because there's just too goddamned
much to say and I think of my boyhood
when I loved to jump into shallow
and muddy ditches with my brothers
who were everything in my world,
and my sisters who were like angels—
even better because they needed
no wings and could endure
our boyhood cruelties and still love
us as much as they loved the pure
blue of the New Mexico sky.
And the song Louis Armstrong
is singing mourns
the passing of summer, wants
to cling to it forever. But I am
wondering at this very moment

if I can endure one more blessèd
second of the summer's heat.

The Ninth Dream:
War (in the City in Which I Live)

All my life—let me say this so you understand—*all my life*
I have heard stories of the river and how people were willing
To die to cross it. To die just to get to other side. The other
Side was the side I lived on. "And people die to get here?"
My mother nodded at my question in that way that told me
She was too busy to discuss the matter and went back
To her ritual of rolling out tortillas for her seven children, some
Of whom asked questions she had no answers for. We were
Poor as a summer without rain; we had an outhouse and a pipe
Bringing in cold water from a well that was unreliable
As the white man's treaties with the Indians, unreliable
As my drunk uncles, unreliable as my father's Studebaker
Truck. I was six. It was impossible for me to fathom
Why anyone would risk death for the chance to live like us.

✳

          I have heard people laugh when
They see the Río Grande for the first time. *That is the river?*
But that river has claimed a thousand lives, Mexicans caught
In its currents mistaking the river as something tame, and in
One second the river devoured them whole. The survivors
Have handed down this lesson: Nothing in the desert is
Tame. Not the people, not the sand, not the winds, not
The sun, not even the river that resembles a large ditch,
That's laughed at by visitors and locals alike. Nothing
In the desert has ever had anything resembling mercy
On Mexicans attempting to leave their land, to become
Something they weren't meant to be.

✳

People are still crossing. People are still dying. Some have
Died suffocating in boxcars. Some have drowned. Some
Have been killed by vigilantes who protect us in the name
Of all that is white. Some have died in a desert larger than
Their dreams. Some were found, no hint of their names
On their remains. In the city that is my home, Border Patrol
Vans are as ubiquitous as taxicabs in New York. Green vans
Are a part of my landscape, a part of my imagination, no less
Than the sky or the river or the ocotillos blooming in spring.
The West is made of things that make you bleed. I no longer
Hang images of summer clouds or Indians carrying pots on their
Talented heads or Mexican peasants working the land with magic
Hands. On my walls, I no longer hang paintings of the Holy Poor.

                    *

                We have been fighting a war on this border
For hundreds of years. We have been fighting the war so long
That the war has become as invisible as the desert sands we
Trample on.

                I do not know how long all this will continue. Peace
Is like the horizon. We can see it in the distance
But it is always far and we can never touch it.

                    *

                                        Every day
In what passes for a newspaper in the city in which
I live, someone writes a letter ranting against the use
Of the Spanish language because this is America, and I can
Taste the hate in the letter, can almost feel the spit
In the letter writer's mouth, and I know we could not
Ever speak about this without one of us wanting to hurt
The other in the city in which I live.

*

I will tell you a sad story: White people are moving away
From this city that has claimed my heart. They are running away
From my people. They are running away from all that keeps
Us poor. I want them to stay and fight. I want them
To stay and live with my people. *We have chased them*
Away. I want them to love the people who make the food
They love. *We have chased them away—are you happy? Are you*
Happy? And there are people waiting in line, spending
Their fortunes just for a chance to enter, waiting, just blocks
Away from where I sit, waiting to come over, waiting in Juárez
Just to cross the river, from China and India and all the nations
Of Africa and Central America and Asia. No poet, no engineer, no
Politician, no philosopher, no artist, no novelist has ever
Dreamed a solution. I am tired of living in exile. I am tired
Of chasing others off the land.

Let me say this again. Again. Again.
I want, I want this war to end. To end.

The Tenth Dream:
This Is How It Will End. Is This How It
Will End?

A phone call in the middle

of the night.

A nurse's panicked voice.

I listen, already knowing
what I have been
expecting—and yet hoping
would never come
(I am as predictable
as every other man
who has ever lived—
hoping and hoping and—)

My heart begins to race. I put
on my pants (the equivalent, I suppose,
of a man putting on his armor
in a small war he has to fight,
a small war he knows will end
in defeat). I sit for a moment
to calm myself as I put on socks
and shoes. I stop and watch
my wife as she, too, readies for what
is coming. We are in this together
and I think to myself I know
nothing of the strangeness
of grief though I know it is written
in my eyes, and know this woman

I love watches for signs
of chaos as she studies me.

As we drive through the night
toward that loved and familiar
city of my youth, that city where
my father spent his life and now
lies dying,
              I try not to think
of a frail man with a tube
forced down his throat.
I try not to think of the litany
of medical conditions
that had begun to devour
my father—*and my mother, too.*
I try to erase all the doctors'
names that are colonizing my memory
as if it were a newly discovered
island: *Reynolds, Iqbal, Richards, Flores.*

                    *

                    As I stare out
at the desert, I refuse to think
of my father in terms of diseases,
medications, doctors. I begin picturing
my father in his many guises—
like John Wayne and Pedro Infante
my father was the star
of every scene.

                    My father's life projects
itself onto my mind and heart
and I become nothing

more than a screen
where the images appear: My father
on a tractor as he plowed the fields,
sweat pouring out of him
as if he was the source
of all the water in the world.
My father skinning a deer
and me still a boy
wondering at the strange cruelty
and treachery of men.
My father frying chicharrones,
stirring the pot on a cold
December day, and how
I'd thought that maybe God
smelled like smoke and chicharrones
and my father. My father sobbing
the day his own mother died, and me
an awkward adolescent
who had no words of comfort.
My father throwing
a shoe at the television
when Reagan (a man he hated
as sure as anyone he had ever, ever
hated) came on the screen. My father
railing against the rich, against
Texas, against a country who loved
slogans and hamburger chains
and salsa and breakfast burritos
more than it would ever love
Mexicans.

　　　As the scenes abandon me
I feel myself to be an orphan, destitute,
alone on an empty street.

I look at my wife as she drives
the car, and her face in the darkness
gives me something that resembles
comfort. I take a breath and it occurs
to me that my father was a large
mesquite with thorns which could
grow through decades of drought,
but his heart yearned for rain
and fields of summer corn. I see
him laughing, no wincing in pain.
I see the man my mother loved. I want
to open the window and yell out
into the desert night: *Do you
know the value of an old tree
in this land that makes
and breaks us all?* I have lived
my life under this tree, and I
do not know what
I will do when the tree is gone.

*

           I watch my brother attempt
to wake my father and stand in wonder
as I listen to him repeat again and again *Do
you hear me, Dad? Do you hear me?* He becomes
an angel of desperate resurrection. I watch
my mother weep—then compose
herself, then weep again. I watch her
lips move in prayer. I watch my sister
and my wife place their arms
around her.
           I make the necessary phone calls.

One by one, my brothers and sisters
gather, a migrating tribe returning
to their originary homeland. In the darkness
of the early morning, when the last son
arrives, I know it is time. I sign
a piece of paper and they remove
the tube. I am no longer myself. I am
now only a watcher who is watching
myself. My father is no longer my father.
The earth is no longer earth. And the names
of the dogs my father loved
and lost appear—then disappear before
they can offer me comfort.

I am no longer who I was.

   I return to my father, and we
watch this patriarch slowly leave
the world. But I, the middle son, never
highly favored as a boy, never unloved
as a man, know my father is already dead.

My father is dead.

    As I drift off
to sleep that morning, in a hotel that has
even less definition than the hollow
tears of grief that surround me, I hear
my father's last breaths in my ear.
I look around in the darkness—
and feel myself drowning in the ocean
of the black and broken night.

*

Every night, now, I dream my father.
I dream his funeral.
I dream his temper. I dream
his kindness, his inability to hold
a grudge. I wake and think
that I do not understand the stranger
who was my father—even in death.
I want to scream in anger
at the father who refused
to speak of his demons—
the secrets he kept closer
to his scarred and bitter heart
than any of his daughters,
than any of his sons.
The dreams come every night.

*

I am cooking dinner and listening
to the news on NPR. The announcer says
another soldier has been killed in Iraq.
I am waiting for peace to arrive.
For the people of the Middle East.
For America. For Mexico. For me.

*

Have we fallen in love with apocalypse?

*

For my father, all wars
have come to an end—
but not for the sons and daughters
he has left behind.

*

My wife is on her way to me
from work. Tonight, a pot of freshly
cooked beans. Green chile and tomatoes.
The radio invades my house
as I shuck the corn. The voices
bring me news of wars in Africa
and Iraq, impending peace between
Israel and the Palestinians.
I stare at the morning paper my wife
left on a counter—another man
dead from trying to get across the river.

*Another man, dead. From trying
to get across the river.*

I do not know how all this will end.

I begin to wonder about the soldier,
my father, the man trying to cross the river.

This is how it will all end. Is this how it will all end?

The Eleventh Dream:
Fathers and Other Gods

August not an hour old—

my father dead.
                    Not one of us
with him as he choked. All
his sons and daughters wrapped
and twisted in the blankets
of uneasy sleep, our dreams
crowded with dark gods prying
open our clenched and calloused
fists, stealing what we cling to.

They take what
they want, those gods,

and leave the rest.

Their insatiable
desire for us
is unending, vile,
violent.

A pig squeals when you shoot it.

Have you ever twisted the head off a chicken?

                    And me, waking,
my hands and lips trembling, the sound
of that goddamned ceaseless ringing

in the middle of the night *Oh do not*
ask for whom the bell and me, at last,

answering that phone without a hint of grace.

*

Death stops the waking
and the dreaming. Death stops
the daily rhythms, the hours
planned, the meals we—

                    you are sitting

on that bed in that hospital gown

you look small and happy tomorrow

you'll be home Mom will cook

something tortillas simple frijoles

you can taste her hands

in the food in your mouth you are

sitting on your front porch the one

you built with your own hands your

dog lying at your feet as you

wait for the mail—

                    but oh my father
death stops nothing of what matters.

As you fall choking fighting
for a breath

        you are home the mail

carrier is coming with some news
that will change everything.

        *

Between one hospital and another,
you came home
        for a night.
              Mom
looking over your medications,
reading each label, scrutinizing
each word, then staring straight
into the contents as if she were
looking into an oracle.
        Dad, you appeared
in the kitchen
        wearing the skin
of a man eroded by pills
and insulin
        and then—with the grace
of a young man diving into a pool,
you took a fork, dug
into an apple pie
and ate like a man ravished
by a hunger that could never be
sated *sugar, sugar, God be an angel*
made of sugar.
        I watched in rage, the doctor's voice
playing in the speakers
installed in my brain *your father*

has to watch, your father has to—I am
still watching myself grabbing that
pie, tossing it in the trash, then
turning, staring you down
like the hundred times you did
the same to me.
I was a worse father to you
than you ever were to me.

✳

The gods

take. Like vultures

they swarm over

your body—

                Dad, what will we

do with their leavings?

The Twelfth and Final Dream:
A Dream of the Day

          The surface of my life is not
a complicated matter. I hear my wife
wake

and listen for the sound
          of running water.
                    Sometimes,
the sound of water on her skin
makes me doze
          in peace
          (I imagine her
bathing in the rain).

          Then the dog disturbs
my thoughts. Seeing that I make a move
to rise, she places her paws
on the bed and barks. She will not be
calmed or satisfied until she feels my hand
upon her head.
          She is addicted
to her morning dose of touch, intelligent
enough to understand my small
yet great affection.
          I smell
the brewing coffee, slip on my jeans
in a stupor,
          then walk out the door
to get the local daily.
          The dog eyes
my steps, watches close, watches, watches

as I open the shutters. I look down
                at this creature, this dog
who looks up at me,
                        and I repeat
my daily phrase:
                "Let in the day. Let in
                        the day."

                I read the paper, curse
the vacuous writing. *This is what*
they choose to print?
                I toss the news aside,
put on my shoes—then leash
the waiting dog.
                        Morning
rituals are common principles
                of order.
                I have grown to love
these simple hours.

I walk the dog. And dream.

The cruelty of the desert
subsides in the early hours
of the day.

                        *

Summers   I plant
and hoe   and garden.
I do   the errands that a house demands.

                        These are simple
things I speak of, the uncomplicated
surfaces of life.

I am not fooled
by my own aesthetics. There are complications
buried just beneath these words.
                On certain days
they threaten me. I will not
speak of them today.

In the age when memoir

rules the page, is it a sin

to keep things out of view?

My private wars are small
but they are mine.

                        *

                Summers, I write.

There are poems in my head, stories,
novels, essays,

                screenplays where protagonists
are as ordinary as the writer. Words clutter
and complicate. They stick in my throat
until I must find a way to clear a path
for air.

                There are moments

when I wander from the writing.

There are things that writing cannot hold.

I stare out and see only
what is in my head. I dream of things
in the day.

    In the day. I dream
that nothing
in my house needs fixing. I dream
the labor it will take to build
a wall—

    then to tear it down.

       I dream
my mother has no worries. She has worked
and suffered enough,

    worked and suffered enough
and it is time for her to rest. And though
I know my father's death cannot be dreamed
away, or my mother's memory, or her pain,
or her bills or her crooked bones—

    this knowing does not stop
me from my dream.

    I dream my mother's young
again. I dream her aging body has no aches.

    I dream my sisters and my brothers
have no debts, and dream

    they have
the time to spend on who and what
they love. I dream abundance
in their lives.

    I dream Eden and a garden
in their hearts.

    I dream. The day.

I dream the poor who come from other lands

will not be sent away. I dream the federal judge

will find an atlas of the world, stand

in awe of their journeys—and wave

them safely in. I dream the day.

I dream that all who left my city

will come back. Exiles returning

to build again what has been

left unbuilt.

I dream. The day. I dream that all

the wars are done. I dream the earth, having lost

all patience, rises up in its own revolution,

erasing all the lines we have carved

on her back. I dream there are no more

nations. This is what I dream—that

nations do not matter.

At this very moment,

I am dreaming. It is still morning

and I have never been more

awake. I am dreaming that my life is coming

to an end. I am an old man and my body

is tired and I am not afraid of turning

into dust. I have lived a good life. I am

lying in a bed and I am telling those

who surround me that I am leaving

them, that they can do what they like

with all the things I loved and leave

behind. And as I die, I see

the resurrection of the animals,

victims of our greed

and gluttonous wars.

As I take my final

breath, I find myself standing

in front of the river. The river I love,

the river of my boyhood, the river

the world mocked. And the river, no

longer poor, is wide and flowing

with water as blue as Adam's sky.

I am looking at the other side,

the side I called Mexico

in life, and see that it is in full

bloom, the paradise I yearned for

all the days I wandered on the earth.

I want to cross the river, but I know

I cannot swim—will drown trying

to reach that holy place. I sit

and mourn. I will spend eternity

in exile. But my dog,

long dead, appears at my side.

I whisper her name and she looks

across the river, then barks. I smile

at her simple speech. I stare across

the river, too, and *there* I see my wife

—my wife and those I loved

and lost and mourned. I see my niece.

She is whole again—and perfect—

and standing next to my sister

and my mother and my father, all

their ailments gone. They are

waving at me. They are calling

my name and I know they forgive me

all my sins. I wave, but wave

in grief. I cannot reach them.

        Then the resurrected

animals encircle me. There are thousands.

There are millions. All the dead animals, all

the animals we killed to build

our kingdoms. They make no

move to harm me—but

I am half afraid. If they choose to

tear me up, and divide my flesh for food,

what could I say to save myself?

        And then the ants begin to crawl

all over me, the welts growing

on my skin like weeds after a rain. My dog,

with one small growl, sends the ants away.

She licks my wounds, then looks into my eyes—

and then she circles me. The animals

fix their eyes on the dance of this dog

I loved so many years ago. And then

she leads me to the water's edge. She pulls

me in. I cling to her as she begins to swim

across the river. She can bear

my weight. This is what I am dreaming.

My dog is carrying me across the river. She can

bear my weight. We are crossing

to the other side. Those who

have crossed before me   await

the arrival of this new immigrant.

About the Author

Benjamin Alire Sáenz, poet and novelist, was born in Las Cruces, New Mexico, in 1954. His first book of poems, *Calendar of Dust*, received an American Book Award in 1991. He has two other collections of poetry, *Dark and Perfect Angels* and *Elegies in Blue*. His works of fiction include *Flowers for the Broken*, *Carry Me Like Water*, *The House of Forgetting*, *Sammy and Juliana in Hollywood*, and the recently published novel *In Perfect Light*. He was a Wallace Stegner Poetry Fellow at Stanford University, and he has won various other awards, including a Lannan Poetry Fellowship, a Southwest Book Award, the Paterson Prize, the Americas Book Award, and has been a finalist for the Los Angeles Times Book Prize. He has also written two children's books, and his third, *A Perfect Season for Dreaming*, will be published in the fall of 2006. He and his wife, Patricia Macias, call the border their home. He teaches in the Creative Writing Department at the University of Texas at El Paso.

This book was designed and typeset by Phil Kovacevich, and printed in the United States by McNaughton & Gunn. The typeface is Centaur. Originally designed by Bruce Rogers for the Metropolitan Museum in 1914, Centaur was released by Monotype in 1929. Modeled on letters cut by the fifteenth-century printer Nicolas Jenson, Centaur has a beauty of line and proportion that has been widely acclaimed since its release.

Copper Canyon Press wishes to acknowledge the support of Lannan Foundation in funding the publication and distribution of exceptional literary works.

LANNAN LITERARY SELECTIONS 2006

Taha Muhammad Ali, *So What: New & Selected Poems*
Madeline DeFrees, *Spectral Waves*
Theodore Roethke, *Straw for the Fire: From the Notebooks of Theodore Roethke*
Benjamin Alire Sáenz, *Dreaming the End of War*
Matthew Zapruder, *The Pajamaist*

LANNAN LITERARY SELECTIONS 2000–2005

John Balaban, *Spring Essence: The Poetry of Hồ Xuân Hương*

Marvin Bell, *Rampant*

Hayden Carruth, *Doctor Jazz*

Cyrus Cassells, *More Than Peace and Cypresses*

Norman Dubie, *The Mercy Seat: Collected & New Poems, 1967–2001*

Sascha Feinstein, *Misterioso*

James Galvin, *X: Poems*

Jim Harrison, *The Shape of the Journey: New and Collected Poems*

June Jordan, *Directed by Desire: The Collected Poems of June Jordan*

Maxine Kumin, *Always Beginning: Essays on a Life in Poetry*

Ben Lerner, *The Lichtenberg Figures*

Antonio Machado, *Border of a Dream: Selected Poems*, translated by Willis Barnstone

W.S. Merwin, *The First Four Books of Poems, Migration: New and Selected Poems, Present Company*

Pablo Neruda, *The Separate Rose, Still Another Day*

Cesare Pavese, *Disaffections: Complete Poems 1930–1950*, translated by Geoffrey Brock

Antonio Porchia, *Voices*, translated by W.S. Merwin

Kenneth Rexroth, *The Complete Poems of Kenneth Rexroth*

Alberto Ríos, *The Smallest Muscle in the Human Body*, *The Theater of Night*

Theodore Roethke, *On Poetry & Craft: Selected Prose of Theodore Roethke*

Ann Stanford, *Holding Our Own: The Selected Poems of Ann Stanford*

Ruth Stone, *In the Next Galaxy*

Joseph Stroud, *Country of Light*

Rabindranath Tagore, *The Lover of God*, translated by Tony K. Stewart and Chase Twichell

Reversible Monuments: Contemporary Mexican Poetry, edited by Mónica de la Torre and Michael Wiegers

César Vallejo, *The Black Heralds*, translated by Rebecca Seiferle

Eleanor Rand Wilner, *The Girl with Bees in Her Hair*

C.D. Wright, *Steal Away: Selected and New Poems*

For more on the Lannan Literary Selections,
visit: www.coppercanyonpress.org

The Chinese character for poetry is made up of two parts: "word" and "temple." It also serves as pressmark for Copper Canyon Press.

Founded in 1972, Copper Canyon Press remains dedicated to publishing poetry exclusively, from Nobel laureates to new and emerging authors. The Press thrives with the generous patronage of readers, writers, book-sellers, librarians, teachers, students, and funders—everyone who shares the conviction that poetry invigorates the language and sharpens our appreciation of the world.

Major funding has been provided by:

Anonymous
The Paul G. Allen Family Foundation
Lannan Foundation
National Endowment for the Arts
Washington State Arts Commission

Copper Canyon Press gratefully
acknowledges Madeleine Wilde,
whose generous Annual Fund support
made publication of this book possible.

For information and catalogs:

COPPER CANYON PRESS
Post Office Box 271
Port Townsend, Washington 98368
360-385-4925
www.coppercanyonpress.org